Modern Chinese (BOOK 1)

– Learn Chinese in a Simple and Successful Way
– Series 1, 2, 3, 4

by Vivienne Zhang

Rebecca

Rong Li

李蓉

ISBN: 1490387668
ISBN-13: 978-1490387666

Acknowledgements

There are many people without whose helpful support and encouragement BOOK 1, 2, 3, 4 would not have become a reality. I would like to express my heartfelt gratitude to my good friend, Pax Webb, for his patience and meticulous care in proofreading the drafts and offering suggestions.

I wish to thank my parents for their undivided support and interest, whose wisdom inspired me and encouraged me to go my own way, without whom I would be unable to complete these books. I am also very grateful to my siblings, especially my younger sister Vicky who shares my daily happiness and woes. My appreciation of their love for me truly goes beyond mere words.

I also give my sincere appreciation to all the teachers who have taught and encouraged me during my life studies. From their instructive courses and stimulating discussions I have acquired many insights and a genuine love for languages and linguistics.

I hope you find these books as interesting, challenging and rewarding as I did writing them.

Preface

In recent years, China has grown to be a powerhouse in the world economy. Mandarin, Putonghua in Chinese, has always been the world's most spoken language by sheer volume of native speakers but its value has also become especially important among foreigners and business professionals. With the ever increasing focus on international trade with China, Western interest in learning Chinese has grown exponentially.

As a Chinese native speaker fluent in English, I have been translating, interpreting and teaching for many years. I have not always been satisfied with the available books and materials for teaching Chinese to foreigners. Over the last several years I have tried, tested and perfected various lessons and techniques that apply well to Chinese studies. I have collected and now publish all of these modern techniques into books.

One of the unique features in these books is the literal translation into English of common Chinese expressions and vocabulary. For example, you can often see "lit." with the grammar points in BOOK 1, showing the direct translation of the Chinese text. This will reinforce an understanding of sentence structure and grammar which has proven to be instrumental in helping you retain the Chinese you have already learned. Other Chinese language books do not use this approach.

In BOOK 1, Part 1 teaches the Chinese Pinyin system, the Romanization of Mandarin, often considered the foundation for learning the language. After Part 1 is completed, you can move on to Part 2 which provides an understanding of grammar points. There are useful examples to help you grasp each of the grammar points. Part 2 is arranged in such a way that any topic in this part can be studied independently.

Upon completion of this book, you will attain mastery of Chinese grammar and vocabulary.

Table of Contents

Part 1   **Pinyin** 7

Charts of Initials and Finals 8

Four Tones 20

Neutral Tone 32

Some Basic Tone Change Rules......................... 35

Part 2   **Grammar Points** 39

Numbers (0-100).. 40

Time 42

Pronouns.. 61

Numbers and Usages.. 77

Measure Words and Money 83

Interrogatives 93

Prepositions.. 116

Conjunctions 131

Adjectives... 149

Comparative Degree of Adjectives................... 157

Superlative Degrees of Adjectives.................... 163

Common Adjectives and Their Related Words 171

Part 1   Pinyin

The Pinyin system is composed of three parts: initials, finals and tones.

Initials are the sounds that come at the beginning of words, finals are the sounds that come at the end of words, and tones describe the level at which those words are spoken. Let's have a closer look.

Charts of Initials and Finals

When first learning how to speak Pinyin, we use the 1st tone to pronounce all initials and finals.

The finals begin with "a", "o", "e":

Finals / Initials	a	o	e	er	ai	ei	ao	ou
b	ba	bo			bai	bei	bao	
p	pa	po			pai	pei	pao	pou
m	ma	mo	me		mai	mei	mao	mou
f	fa	fo				fei		fou
d	da		de		dai	dei	dao	dou
t	ta		te		tai	tei	tao	tou
n	na		ne		nai	nei	nao	nou

	a		e		ai	ei	ao	ou
l	la		le		lai	lei	lao	lou
g	ga		ge		gai	gei	gao	gou
k	ka		ke		kai	kei	kao	kou
h	ha		he		hai	hei	hao	hou
j								
q								
x								
zh	zha		zhe		zhai	zhei	zhao	zhou
ch	cha		che		chai		chao	chou
sh	sha		she		shai	shei	shao	shou
r			re				rao	rou
z	za		ze		zai	zei	zao	zou
c	ca		ce		cai		cao	cou
s	sa		se		sai		sao	sou

Finals Initials	an	en	ang	eng	ong	-i
b	ban	ben	bang	beng		
p	pan	pen	pang	peng		
m	man	men	mang	meng		
f	fan	fen	fang	feng		
d	dan	den	dang	deng	dong	
t	tan		tang	teng	tong	
n	nan	nen	nang	neng	nong	
l	lan		lang	leng	long	
g	gan	gen	gang	geng	gong	
k	kan	ken	kang	keng	kong	
h	han	hen	hang	heng	hong	
j						
q						

x						
zh	zhan	zhen	zhang	zheng	zhong	zhi
ch	chan	chen	chang	cheng	chong	chi
sh	shan	shen	shang	sheng		shi
r	ran	ren	rang	reng	rong	ri
z	zan	zen	zang	zeng	zong	zi
c	can	cen	cang	ceng	cong	ci
s	san	sen	sang	seng	song	si

Note 1: After zh, ch, sh, z, c, s, and r, "i" is not pronounced.

The finals begin with "i":

Finals / Initials	i	ia	ie	iao	iou(iu)
b	bi		bie	biao	
p	pi		pie	piao	
m	mi		mie	miao	miu
f					
d	di	dia	die	diao	diu
t	ti		tie	tiao	
n	ni		nie	niao	niu
l	li	lia	lie	liao	liu
g					
k					
h					
j	ji	jia	jie	jiao	jiu

q	qi	qia	qie	qiao	qiu
x	xi	xia	xie	xiao	xiu
zh					
ch					
sh					
r					
z					
c					
s					
	yi	ya	ye	yao	you

Note 2: "y" is not an initial. It is a Pinyin symbol of "i".

Finals Initials	ian	in	ing	iang	iong
b	bian	bin	bing		
p	pian	pin	ping		
m	mian	min	ming		
f					
d	dian		ding		
t	tian		ting		
n	nian	nin	ning	niang	
l	lian	lin	ling	liang	
g					
k					
h					
j	jian	jin	jing	jiang	jiong
q	qian	qin	qing	qiang	qiong

x	xian	xin	xing	xiang	xiong
zh					
ch					
sh					
r					
z					
c					
s					
	yan	yin	ying	yang	yong

Note 3: yan is from y(i)an, so pay attention to the pronunciation.

The finals begin with "u" and "ü":

Finals / Initials	u	ua	uo	uai	uei(ui)
b	bu				
p	pu				
m	mu				
f	fu				
d	du		duo		dui
t	tu		tuo		tui
n	nu		nuo		
l	lu		luo		
g	gu	gua	guo	guai	gui
k	ku	kua	kuo	kuai	kui
h	hu	hua	huo	huai	hui
j					

q					
x					
zh	zhu	zhua	zhuo	zhuai	zhui
ch	chu	chua	chuo	chuai	chui
sh	shu	shua	shuo	shuai	shui
r	ru	rua	ruo		rui
z	zu		zuo		zui
c	cu		cuo		cui
s	su		suo		sui
	wu	wa	wo	wai	wei

Note 4: "w" is not an initial, same as "y" in the previous charts. It's a Pinyin symbol of "u".

Finals / Initials	uan	uen (un)	uang	ueng	ü	üe	üan	ün
b								
p								
m								
f								
d	duan	dun						
t	tuan	tun						
n	nuan				nü	nüe		
l	luan	lun			lü	lüe		
g	guan	gun	guang					
k	kuan	kun	kuang					
h	huan	hun	huang					
j					ju	jue	juan	jun
q					qu	que	quan	qun

x						xu	xue	xuan	xun
zh	zhuan	zhun	zhuang						
ch	chuan	chun	chuang						
sh	shuan	shun	shuang						
r	ruan	run							
z	zuan	zun							
c	cuan	cun							
s	suan	sun							
	wan	wen	wang	weng	yu	yue	yuan	yun	

Note 5: After "j", "q", "x", "y", the two dots on "ü" are omitted, but the pronunciation is still "ü".

Four Tones

There are four tones in the Pinyin system. They are the 1st tone " ¯ ", the 2nd tone " ´ ", the 3rd tone " ˇ ", and the 4th tone " ` ". Tones can literally change the meaning of the words. With different tones, sometimes the meanings can be opposite, e.g. mǎi (buy) and mài (sell). Make sure you know the tones very well before you progress to the next part.

a: ā, á, ǎ, à

mā, wá, mǎ, bà

妈, 娃, 马, 爸

o: ō, ó, ǒ, ò

bō, bó, wǒ, wò

播, 伯, 我, 卧

e: ē, é, ě, è

gē, hé, kě, kè

哥, 和, 可, 客

i: ī, í, ǐ, ì

yī, mí, xǐ, mì

衣, 谜, 喜, 蜜

u: ū, ú, ǔ, ù

gū, zú, tǔ, kù

姑, 足, 土, 裤

ü: ǖ, ǘ, ǚ, ǜ

jū, yú, nǚ, lǜ

居, 鱼, 女, 绿

Usually the tones are marked above the finals: "a", "o", "e", "i", "u", "ü". In case two finals appear in the same syllable, the tone should be marked on only one, selected by the following order: (1) "a"; (2) "o" or "e"; (3) "i", "u", "ü". When "i" and "u" appear together, the tone is put on the latter one.

e.g.

xiān, cái, zǎo, qià

gòu, guò

fēi, qiè

nüè, lüè, quē, yuán

xiū, jiǔ

duì, huì

The most common Mandarin words are comprised of two syllables.

Practice these words with 1st and 1st tones:

参加 cānjiā (join)

声音 shēngyīn (sound)

西瓜 xīguā (watermelon)

担心 dānxīn (worry)

飞机 fēijī (airplane)

冬天 dōngtiān (winter)

Practice these words with 1st and 2nd tones :

刚才 gāngcái (just now)

欢迎 huānyíng (welcome)

心情 xīnqíng (mood)

工人 gōngrén (worker)

聪明 cōngmíng (clever/smart)

咨询 zīxún (consult)

Practice these words with 1st and 3rd tones:

温暖 wēnnuǎn (warm)

思想 sīxiǎng (thought)

开始 kāishǐ (start)

方法 fāngfǎ (method)

缺少 quēshǎo (lack of)

机场 jīchǎng (airport)

Practice these words with 1st and 4th tones:

波浪 bōlàng (wave)

方向 fāngxiàng (direction)

音乐 yīnyuè (music)

知道 zhīdào (know)

帮助 bāngzhù (help)

高兴 gāoxìng (happy)

Practice these words with 2nd and 1st tones:

时间 shíjiān (time)

白天 báitiān (day time)

南方 nánfāng (southern)

国家 guójiā (country)

房东 fángdōng (landlord)

成功 chénggōng (success)

Practice these words with 2nd and 2nd tones:

男人 nánrén (man)

足球 zúqiú (football)

严格 yángé (strict)

长城 chángchéng (Great Wall)

银行 yínháng (bank)

和平 hépíng (peace)

Practice these words with 2nd and 3rd tones:

谜语 míyǔ (riddle)

如果 rúguǒ (if)

平等 píngděng (equality)

牛奶 niúnǎi (milk)

结果 jiéguǒ (result)

词典 cídiǎn (dictionary)

Practice these words with 2nd and 4th tones:

头发 tóufà (hair)

节日 jiérì (festival)

责任 zérèn (responsibility)

联系 liánxì (contact)

名片 míngpiàn (business card)

愉快 yúkuài (pleasure)

Practice these words with 3rd and 1st tones:

点心 diǎnxīn (dim sum)

烤鸭 kǎoyā (roast duck)

老师 lǎoshī (teacher)

每天 měi tiān (every day)

组织 zǔzhī (organize)

取消 qǔxiāo (cancel)

Practice these words with 3rd and 2nd tones:

语言 yǔyán (language)

海洋 hǎiyáng (ocean)

女人 nǚrén (woman)

起床 qǐchuáng (get up)

旅游 lǚyóu (travel)

解决 jiějué (solve)

Practice these words with 3rd and 3rd tones (the first 3rd tone turns into 2nd tone):

老板 lǎobǎn (boss)

你好 nǐ hǎo (hello)

手表 shǒubiǎo (watch)

舞蹈 wǔdǎo (dance, as a noun)

友好 yǒuhǎo (friendly)

永远 yǒngyuǎn (forever)

Practice these words with 3rd and 4th tones:

跑步 pǎobù (go running)

可爱 kě'ài (cute/lovely)

米饭 mǐfàn (cooked rice)

考虑 kǎolǜ (think about)

酒店 jiǔdiàn (hotel)

准备 zhǔnbèi (prepare)

Practice these words with 4th and 1st tones:

闹钟 nàozhōng (alarm clock)

耐心 nàixīn (patient)

健康 jiànkāng (healthy)

律师 lǜshī (lawyer)

唱歌 chànggē (sing)

放松 fàngsōng (relax)

Practice these words with 4th and 2nd tones:

发型 fàxíng (hairstyle)

热情 rèqíng (passionate)

内容 nèiróng (contents)

自由 zìyóu (freedom)

地球 dìqiú (earth)

性格 xìnggé (personality)

Practice these words with 4th and 3rd tones:

报纸 bàozhǐ (newspaper)

自己 zìjǐ (self)

课本 kèběn (textbook)

跳舞 tiàowǔ (dance, as a verb)

父母 fùmǔ (parents)

遛狗 liùgǒu (walk the dog)

Practice these words with 4th and 4th tones:

任务 rènwù (task)

会议 huìyì (meeting)

护照 hùzhào (passport)

计划 jìhuà (plan)

现在 xiànzài (now)

散步 sànbù (take a walk)

Neutral Tone

If there is no tone mark over the final, it means that it is a neutral tone. The common syllables with neutral tone are: "le", "de", "ge", "zi", "men", and "ma". These syllables lose their original tones and are pronounced soft and short.

e.g.

They went to school.: tāmen qù xuéxiào le. 他们去学校了。

He came home.: tā huíjiā le. 他回家了。

Ok: hǎo de 好的

my: wǒ de 我的

this one: zhè ge 这个

one orange: yí ge chéngzi 一个橙子

child: háizi 孩子

example: lìzi 例子

we: wǒmen 我们

they: tāmen 他们

you (plural): nǐmen 你们

Yes?: shì ma? 是吗？

Really?: zhēnde ma? 真的吗？

Do you live in China?: nǐ zhù zài zhōngguó ma? 你住在中国吗？

When the second syllable is a repetition of the first syllable, the second one is almost always pronounced in a neutral tone.

e.g.

Mrs./wife: tàitai 太太

younger sister: mèimei 妹妹

older sister: jiějie 姐姐

younger brother: dìdi 弟弟

older brother: gēge 哥哥

have a look (quick): kànkan 看看

have a try (quick): shìshi 试试

However, this tone change does not occur in Taiwan, where all syllables maintain their original tones. In fact, in daily life Chinese people often speak with the original tones. To keep the Chinese learning process easier, you can speak all neutral syllables with the original tone.

Some Basic Tone Change Rules

1.

Tone change in the 3rd tone.

(1) When two 3rd tones appear together in a two-syllable word, the first 3rd tone should be pronounced as a 2nd tone.

brave: yǒnggǎn (yónggǎn) 勇敢

friendly: yǒuhǎo (yóuhǎo) 友好

manage: guǎnlǐ (guánlǐ) 管理

vote: xuǎnjǔ (xuánjǔ) 选举

so: suǒyǐ (suóyǐ) 所以

(2) When there are three consecutive 3rd tones in a word or phrase, the second 3rd tone should be pronounced as a 2nd tone.

I want to buy: wǒ xiǎng mǎi (wǒ xiáng mǎi) 我想买

I also go: wǒ yě zǒu (wǒ yé zǒu) 我也走

I am well: wǒ hěn hǎo (wǒ hén hǎo) 我很好

I can: wǒ kěyǐ (wǒ kéyǐ) 我可以

2.

Tone change in the negative word "bù" 不

When "bù" occurs before a word with a 4th tone, it changes to the 2nd tone, "bù" becomes "bú". "bù" maintains the 4th tone when it precedes a 1st, 2nd or 3rd tone.

not correct/right: bù duì (bú duì) 不对

not enough: bù gòu (bú gòu) 不够

not important: bù zhòngyào (bú zhòngyào) 不重要

don't need: bù yòng (bú yòng) 不用

don't go: bù qù (bú qù) 不去

3.

Tone change in the word "yī" 一

" yī" (one) takes the 1st tone when used by itself. When " yī" precedes a 1st, 2nd or 3rd tone, it will change to the 4th tone, " yī" becomes " yì". When " yī" occurs before a 4th tone, it will change to a 2nd tone, " yī" becomes " yí".

One: yī 一 / 1

together: yīqǐ (yìqǐ) 一起

a little: yīdiǎn (yìdiǎn) 一点

so-so: yībān (yìbān) 一般

one sheet (e.g. of paper): yī zhāng (yì zhāng) 一张

one thin strip (e.g. of street): yī tiáo (yì tiáo) 一条

one bowl: yī wǎn (yì wǎn) 一碗

a little while: yī huì (yí huì) 一会

all together: yīgòng (yígòng) 一共

certainly: yīdìng (yídìng) 一定

a life time: yī bèizi (yí bèizi) 一辈子

Part 2   Grammar Points

Numbers (0-100)

líng

0

yī, èr, sān, sì, wǔ, liù, qī, bā, jiǔ, shí

1, 2, 3 , 4, 5, 6, 7, 8, 9, 10

shíyī, shí'èr, shísān… èrshí

11, 12,13…20

èrshíyī, èrshí'èr, èrshísān…sānshí

21, 22, 23…30

sānshíyī, sānshí'èr, sānshísān…sìshí

31, 32, 33…40

sìshíyī, sìshí'èr, sìshísān…wǔshí

41, 42, 43…50

wǔshíyī, wǔshí'èr, wǔshísān…liùshí

51, 52, 53…60

liùshíyī, liùshí'èr, liùshísān…qīshí

61, 62, 63…70

qīshíyī, qīshí'èr, qīshísān…bāshí

71, 72, 73…80

bāshíyī, bāshí'èr, bāshísān…jiǔshí

81, 82, 83…90

jiǔshíyī, jiǔshí'èr, jiǔshísān…yìbǎi

91, 92, 93…100

Time

1.

O'clock: diǎn(zhōng) 点(钟)

time: shíjiān 时间

hour: xiǎoshí 小时

leo

6 hours: liù ge xiǎoshí 六个小时

o'clock: …diǎn(zhōng) …点(钟)

chee

7 o'clock: qī diǎn(zhōng) 七点(钟)

half
semi-incomplete

half: bàn 半 *5 strokes*

丶 丶 丷 ⺷ 半

10:30: shí diǎn bàn 十点半

quarter (hour)
moment
to carve, to cut) oppresive

quarter: kè 刻

minute: fēn(zhōng) 分(钟)

o'clock
dot
drop
speck
to draw
to check on list

3:15: sān diǎn yí kè 三点一刻

丨 ⺊ ⺊ 占 占 占 点 点

点

3:15: sān diǎn shíwǔ fēn 三点十五分

second: miǎo 秒

20 seconds: èrshí miǎo 二十秒

a.m./early morning: zǎoshàng 早上

a.m./late morning: shàngwǔ 上午

p.m./noon: zhōngwǔ 中午 ——————— *noon; midday*

p.m./afternoon: xiàwǔ 下午 *4 strokes*

3 strokes

[一 丁 下] 午 [ノ 一 二 午]

p.m./evening/night: wǎnshàng 晚上

7:30a.m.: zǎoshàng qī diǎn bàn 早上七点半

(lit. a.m./early morning 7 o'clock half)

10:15a.m.: shàngwǔ shí diǎn yí kè 上午十点一刻

(lit. a.m./late morning 10 o'clock 1 quarter)

12:30p.m.: zhōngwǔ shí'èr diǎn bàn 中午十二点半

(lit. p.m./noon 12 o'clock half)

1p.m.: xiàwǔ yī diǎn 下午一点

(lit. p.m./afternoon 1 o'clock)

8:15p.m.: wǎnshàng bā diǎn shíwǔ fēn 晚上八点十五分

(lit. p.m./evening/night 8 o'clock 15 minutes)

10:05p.m.: wǎnshàng shí diǎn líng wǔ fēn 晚上十点零五分

(lit. p.m./evening/night 10 o'clock 0 5 minutes)

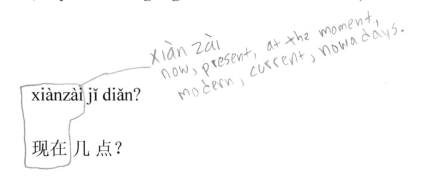

xiànzài jǐ diǎn?

现在 几 点？

What time is it now?

(lit. Now how many o'clock?)

sān diǎn bàn

三 点 半。

Half past three.

(lit. Three o'clock half.)

2.

Eating and Drinking : chī hé hē 吃和喝

I: wǒ 我

drink: hē 喝
to drink
my goodness!

eat: chī 吃

cooked rice: fàn 饭
fàn
food
cuisine
cooked rice
meal

have a meal: chīfàn 吃饭
chī fàn
to eat
to have meal
to make a living

breakfast: zǎofàn 早饭
zǎo
early
morning
Good Morning

coffee: kāfēi 咖啡

lunch: wǔfàn 午饭
nǐ chī wǔfàn

tea: chá 茶
tea
tea plant.

dinner/supper: wǎnfàn 晚饭

Morning I eat breakfast

[zǎoshàng] wǒ chī [zǎofàn.]

早上 我 吃 早饭。

I have breakfast in the morning.

(*lit. Early morning I eat breakfast.*)

I

Late Morning / Drink — coffee

[shàngwǔ] wǒ hē kāfēi

上午 我 喝 咖啡。

I drink coffee in the morning.

(lit. Late morning I drink coffee.)

zhōngwǔ wǒ chī [wǔfàn]

noon   Lunch

[中午] 我 吃 [午饭。]   吃 = eat

At noon I have (eat) lunch.

xiàwǔ wǒ hē chá

afternoon

下午 我 喝 茶。

In the afternoon I drink tea.

in the evening

wǎnshàng wǒ chī wǎnfàn.

晚上 我 吃 晚饭。

In the evening I have (eat) dinner.

3.

Date, Week, Month and Year: hào, xīngqī, yuè hé nián 号、星期、月和年

date: hào/rì 号/日   号

5th: wǔ hào 五号

12th: shí'èr hào 十二号

31st: sānshíyí hào 三十一号

week: xīngqī 星期

Monday: xīngqī yī 星期一

Tuesday: xīngqī èr 星期二

Wednesday: xīngqī sān 星期三

Thursday: xīngqī sì 星期四

Friday: xīngqī wǔ 星期五

Saturday: xīngqī liù 星期六

Sunday: xīngqī tiān 星期天

4 strokes

月 丿 冂 月 月

month: yuè 月

moon
month
monthly, fullmoon

January: yí yuè 一月

February: èr yuè 二月

March: sān yuè 三月

April: sì yuè 四月

May: wǔ yuè 五月

June: liù yuè 六月

July: qī yuè 七月

August: bā yuè 八月

September: jiǔ yuè 九月

October: shí yuè 十月

November: shíyī yuè 十一月

December: shí'èr yuè 十二月

year: nián 年 年 年 年 年 [6 strokes ノ ㇒ ㇒ ㇒ ㇒ 年]

1868: yībāliùbā nián 一八六八年

1953: yījiǔwǔsān nián 一九五三年

2000: èrlínglínglíng nián 二零零零年

2011: èrlíngyīyī nián 二零一一年

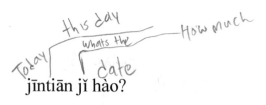

jīntiān jǐ hào?

今天 几 号？ 今天 (today)

What's the date today?

(lit. Today how many date?)

jīntiān èrshíyī hào.

今天 21 号。

Today is the 21st.

(lit. Today 21 date.)

jīntiān xīngqī jǐ?

今天 星期 几？

What (week) day is it today?

(lit. Today week how many?)

50

jīntiān xīngqī èr.

今天 星期 二。

Today is Tuesday.

(lit. Today Tuesday.)

jīntiān shì èrlíngyī'èr nián sān yuè wǔ hào.

今天 是 二 零 一 二 年 三 月 五 号。

Today is March 5th, 2012.

(lit. Today is 2012 year 3 month 5 date.)

Note: When describing a length of time using **year, month, week, or day**, the two in the middle (month and week) require the measure word "ge" while the longest (year) and shortest (day) don't need a measure word.

ten years: shí nián 十年

eight months: bā ge yuè 八个月

August: bā yuè 八月

five weeks: wǔ ge xīngqī 五个星期

three days: sān tiān 三天

4.

Past, Present/Now and Future: guòqù, xiànzài hé jiānglái 过去、现在和将来

Past: guòqù 过去

the day before yesterday: qiántiān 前天

yesterday: zuótiān 昨天

yesterday early morning: zuótiān zǎoshàng 昨天早上

yesterday late morning: zuótiān shàngwǔ 昨天上午

yesterday noon: zuótiān zhōngwǔ 昨天中午

yesterday afternoon: zuótiān xiàwǔ 昨天下午

yesterday evening: zuótiān wǎnshàng 昨天晚上

last year *(lit. go/gone year)*: qùnián 去年

last year February: qùnián èr yuè 去年二月

(with measure word "ge")

last week: shàng ge xīngqī 上个星期

last Monday: shàng ge xīngqī yī 上个星期一

last month: shàng ge yuè 上个月

(with measure word "cì")

last time: shàng cì 上次

Present/Now: xiànzài 现在

today: jīntiān 今天

this early morning: jīntiān zǎoshàng 今天早上

this late morning: jīntiān shàngwǔ 今天上午

this noon: jīntiān zhōngwǔ 今天中午

this afternoon: jīntiān xiàwǔ 今天下午

tonight: jīntiān wǎnshàng 今天晚上

this year: jīnnián 今年

this year June: jīnnián liù yuè 今年六月

(with measure word "ge")

this week: zhè ge xīngqī 这个星期

this Wednesday: zhè ge xīngqī sān 这个星期三

this month: zhè ge yuè 这个月

(with measure word "cì")

this time: zhè cì 这次

Future: jiānglái 将来

the day after tomorrow: hòutiān 后天

tomorrow: míngtiān 明天

tomorrow early morning: míngtiān zǎoshàng 明天早上

tomorrow late morning: míngtiān shàngwǔ 明天上午

tomorrow noon: míngtiān zhōngwǔ 明天中午

tomorrow afternoon: míngtiān xiàwǔ 明天下午

tomorrow evening: míngtiān wǎnshàng 明天晚上

next year: míngnián 明年

next year September: míngnián jiǔ yuè 明年九月

(with measure word "ge")

next week: xià ge xīngqī 下个星期

next Friday: xià ge xīngqī wǔ 下个星期五

next month: xià ge yuè 下个月

(with measure word "cì")

next time: xià cì 下次

5.

Time in Sentences: shíjiān zài jù zhōng de wèizhì 时间在句中的位置

(1) A point in time such as "one year ago", "yesterday" and "three days later" can be placed either before or after the subject of the sentence.

shàng ge xīngqī nǐ qù xī'ān le ma?

上 个 星 期 你 去 西 安 了 吗？

= nǐ shàng ge xīngqī qù xī'ān le ma?

= 你 上 个 星 期 去 西 安 了 吗？

Did you go to Xi'an last week?

(lit. Last week you went Xi'an? = You last week went Xi'an?)

shàng ge xīngqī wǒ méiyǒu qù xī'ān.

上 个 星期 我 没有 去 西安。

= wǒ shàng ge xīngqī méiyǒu qù xī'ān.

= 我 上 个 星期 没有 去 西安。

I didn't go to Xi'an last week.

(lit. Last week I didn't go Xi'an. = I last week didn't go Xi'an.)

míngtiān tā qù xuéxiào ma?

明天 他 去 学校 吗？

= tā míngtiān qù xuéxiào ma?

= 他 明天 去 学校 吗？

Will he go to school tomorrow?

(lit. Tomorrow he goes school? = He tomorrow goes school?)

míngtiān tā bú qù xuéxiào.

明天 他 不 去 学校。

= tā míngtiān bú qù xuéxiào

= 他 明天 不 去 学校。

He will not go to school tomorrow.

(lit. Tomorrow he will not go school. = He tomorrow will not go school.)

Note: did not: méiyǒu 没有 / méi 没

will not: bù / bú 不

(refer to BOOK 2 "Common Verbs and Their Usages" 3 (2))

(2) When a period of time such as "five days", "two months" or "six years" is used in an affirmative sentence, it should be put at the end.

tāmen zài zhōngguó zhù le wǔ nián.

他们 在 中国 住 了 五 年。

They have been living in China for five years.

(lit. They in China lived five years.)

wǒ huì zài běijīng dāi yí ge yuè.

我 会 在 北京 呆 一 个 月。

I will stay in Beijing for one month.

(lit. I will in Beijing stay one month.)

(3) If a period of time such as "five days", "two months" or "a long time" is used in a negative context, it should be put before the verb.

wǒ bànnián méiyǒu kàndào nǐ le.

我 半 年 没有 看到 你 了。

I haven't seen you for half a year.

(lit. I half a year haven't seen you.)

tāmen hěnjiǔ méi lái zhèlǐ le.

他们 很久 没 来 这里 了。

They haven't come here for a long time.

(lit. They long time haven't come here.)

Pronouns

1.

Some/A few: yìxiē 一些

This: zhè 这

That: nà 那

These: zhèxiē 这些

Those: nàxiē 那些

tāmen yǒu yìxiē zhōngguó péngyǒu.

他们 有 一些 中国 朋友。

They have some Chinese friends.

zhè shì yí ge hǎo xuéxiào.

这 是 一 个 好 学校。

This is a good school.

wǒ xǐhuān zhè ge fángzi.

我 喜欢 这 个 房子。

I like this house.

nà shì shénme?

那 是 什么？

What is that?

(lit. That is what?)

nàxiē shì tā de shū.

那些 是 她 的 书。

Those are her books.

zhèxiē tiān wǒ hěn máng.

这些天我很忙。

I am very busy these days.

(lit. These days I very busy.)

2.

I/Me: wǒ 我

You: nǐ 你

He/Him / She/Her / It/It: tā 他 / 她 / 它

wǒ huì bāng(zhù) nǐ.

我 会 帮（助） 你。

I will help you.

qǐng gěi tā zhè zhī bǐ.

请 给 她 这 支 笔。

Please give her the pen.

tā shì wǒ de lǎoshī

他 是 我 的 老师。

He is my teacher.

3.

The plural of a personal pronoun or human-related noun is formed by adding **"men"** after the singular.

we/us: wǒmen 我们

you (plural): nǐmen 你们

they/them: tāmen 他们 / 她们 / 它们

men: nánrénmen 男人们

women: nǚrénmen 女人们

boys: nánháizimen 男孩子们

girls: nǚháizimen 女孩子们

children: háizimen 孩子们

students: xuéshēngmen 学生们

colleagues: tóngshìmen 同事们

workers: gōngrénmen 工人们

friends: péngyǒumen 朋友们

tāmen yìqǐ gōngzuò.

他们 一起 工作。

They work together.

(lit. They together work.)

nǚháizimen xǐhuān guàngjiē.

女孩子们 喜欢 逛街。

Girls like going shopping.

Note: If there is a number in front of a noun, there is no need to add "men". e.g. liǎng ge péngyou (two friends)

4.

Possessive pronouns:

my/mine: wǒ de 我的

your/yours: nǐ de 你的

his/his / her/hers / its/its: tā de 他的 / 她的 / 它的

our/ours: wǒmen de 我们的

your/yours: nǐmen de 你们的

their/theirs: tāmen de 他们的 / 她们的 / 它们的

tā shì wǒ de mèimei.

她 是 我 的 妹妹。

She is my younger sister.

wǒmen de yīngyǔ lǎoshī shì měiguórén.

我们 的 英语 老师 是 美国人。

Our English teacher is an American.

zhèxiē chéngzi shì nǐmen de.

这些 橙子 是 你们 的。

These oranges are yours.

5.

Self : zìjǐ 自己

myself: wǒ zìjǐ 我自己

ourselves: wǒmen zìjǐ 我们自己

yourself: nǐ zìjǐ 你自己

yourselves: nǐmen zìjǐ 你们自己

himself / herself / itself: tā zìjǐ 他自己 / 她自己 / 它自己

themselves: tāmen zìjǐ 他们自己 / 她们自己 / 它们自己

selfish: zìsī 自私

tā zìjǐ huíqù le.

她 自己 回去 了。

She went back by herself.

(lit. She herself went back.)

nǐ yīnggāi zhàogù hǎo nǐ zìjǐ.

你 应该 照顾 好 你 自己。

You should take care of yourself.

(lit. You should take care good yourself.)

yìxiē rén bù zūnzhòng tāmen zìjǐ.

一些 人 不 尊重 他们 自己。

Some people don't respect themselves.

tāmen fēicháng zìsī.

他们 非常 自私。

They are very selfish.

6.

Every: měi 每

every time: měi cì 每次

every day: měi tiān 每天

every week: měi ge xīngqī 每个星期

every month: měi ge yuè 每个月

every year: měi nián 每年

everybody: měi ge rén 每个人

everything: měi jiàn shìqíng 每件事情

every place: měi ge dìfāng 每个地方

měi cì wǒ zài běijīng, wǒ (dōu) qù zhè ge cāntīng.

每次我在北京，我 (都) 去这个餐厅。

Every time I am in Beijing, I go to this restaurant.

tāmen měi tiān hē kāfēi.

他们每天喝咖啡。

They drink coffee every day.

(lit. They every day drink coffee.)

wǒ měi ge yuè chūchāi.

我 每 个 月 出差。

I go on business trips every month.

(lit. I every month go on business trips.)

7.

Any: rènhé 任何

anybody/anyone: rènhé rén 任何人

anytime: rènhé shíhòu 任何时候

anywhere / any place: rènhé dìfāng 任何地方

any (one) day: rènhé yì tiān 任何一天

any problem: rènhé wèntí 任何问题

rènhé rén dōu kěyǐ qù ma?

任何 人 都 可以 去 吗?

Can anyone go?

(lit. Anyone all can go?)

rènhé shíhòu nǐ dōu kěyǐ gěi wǒ dǎ diànhuà.

任何 时候 你 都 可以 给 我 打 电话。

You can call me anytime.

(lit. Anytime you all can to/give me hit phone.)

rènhé yì tiān nǐ dōu kěyǐ ma?

任何 一 天 你 都 可以 吗?

Is any day ok with you?

(lit. Any one day you all ok?)

8.

Another: lìng yī 另一

another person: lìng yí ge rén 另一个人

another meeting: lìng yí ge huìyì 另一个会议

another thing: lìng yí jiàn shìqíng 另一件事情

another building: lìng yí dòng/zuò lóu 另一栋/座楼

lìng yí ge tóngshì zài bàngōngshì.

另一个同事在办公室。

Another colleague is at the office.

jīntiān xiàwǔ wǒ yǒu lìng yí ge huìyì.

今天下午我有另一个会议。

I will have another meeting this afternoon.

(lit. Today afternoon I have another meeting.)

wǒ xiǎng gàosù nǐ lìng yí jiàn shìqíng.

我 想 告诉 你 另 一 件 事情。

I want to tell you another thing.

tā zhù zài lìng yí dòng lóu.

她 住 在 另 一 栋 楼。

She lives in another building.

9.

Other/Else: bié de 别的 / qítā de 其他/它的

hái yǒu bié de / qítā de shìqíng ma?

还 有 别 的 / 其它 的 事情 吗?

Anything else?

(lit: Still have other things?)

tāmen rènshí qítā de rén.

他们 认识 其他 的 人。

They know other people.

10.

Each other: hùxiāng 互相 / bǐcǐ 彼此

wǒmen hùxiāng xuéxí.

我们 互相 学习。

We learn from each other.

(lit. We each other learn.)

tāmen bǐcǐ bú rènshí.

他们 彼此 不 认识。

They don't know each other.

(lit. They each other don't know.)

Exception: bǐcǐ and xiāng (short for hùxiāng) appear in one sentence.

tāmen bǐcǐ xiāng ài.

他们 彼此 相 爱。

They love each other.

(lit. They each other each other love.)

Numbers and Usages

1.

Numbers larger than 100: dà yú yìbǎi de shùzì 大于一百的数字

101: yìbǎi líng yī 一百零一

103: yìbǎi líng sān 一百零三

113: yìbǎi yīshísān 一百一十三

122: yìbǎi èrshí'èr 一百二十二

500: wǔbǎi 五百

1,000: yìqiān 一千

3,000: sānqiān 三千

10,000 (1,0000): yíwàn 一万

60,000 (6,0000): liùwàn 六万

100,000 (10,0000): shíwàn 十万

1,000,000 (100,0000): yìbǎiwàn 一百万

2.

In Chinese, no matter how many zeroes are between two positive integers (numbers 1-9), they are read as only one zero.

505: wǔbǎi líng wǔ 五百零五

1,005: yìqiān líng wǔ 一千零五

1,050: yìqiān líng wǔshí 一千零五十

10,006: yíwàn líng liù 一万零六

10,600: yíwàn líng liùbǎi 一万零六百

10,605: yíwàn líng liùbǎi líng wǔ 一万零六百零五

3.

Two: liǎng 两

"liǎng" is commonly used before measure words such as "ge", "jīn" and "běn", and before nouns indicating money, time, etc.

two people: liǎng ge rén 两个人

two *jin* (= one kilo) oranges: liǎng jīn chéngzi 两斤橙子

two books: liǎng běn shū 两本书

two o'clock: liǎng diǎn(zhōng) 两点(钟)

two *yuan*: liǎng yuán 两元 / liǎng kuài(qián) 两块(钱)

4.

Ordinal numbers: xùshùcí 序数词

"dì" precedes numbers to form ordinal numbers. A measure word is always required to follow the ordinal numbers.

1st: dì yī 第一

2nd: dì èr 第二

3rd: dì sān 第三

4th: dì sì 第四

5th: dì wǔ 第五

nà shì wǒ dì yī cì jiàndào tā.

那 是 我 第 一 次 见到 他。

That was the first time I saw him.

(lit. That was I first time saw him.)

zhè shì wǒ dì sān cì lái zhōngguó.

这 是 我 第 三 次 来 中国。

This is the third time I have come to China.

(lit. This is I third time come China.)

tā shì wǒ dì èr ge dìdi.

他 是 我 第 二 个 弟弟。

He is my second younger brother.

5.

Fractions: fēnshù 分数

Chinese fractions are expressed in the opposite way to English. The denominator comes first.

1/2: èr fēn zhī yī 二分之一

1/5: wǔ fēn zhī yī 五分之一

3/5: wǔ fēn zhī sān 五分之三

7/10: shí fēn zhī qī 十分之七

6.

Percent: bǎi fēn zhī 百分之

80 percent (80/100): bǎi fēn zhī bāshí 百分之八十

65 percent (65/100): bǎi fēn zhī liùshíwǔ 百分之六十五

bǎi fēn zhī jiǔshí de rén tóngyì tā de guāndiǎn.

百 分 之 九 十 的 人 同 意 他 的 观 点。

90 percent of people agree with his opinions.

7.

Decimals: xiǎoshù 小数

"diǎn" is used to express the decimal point.

0.8: líng diǎn bā 零点八

12.59: shí'èr diǎn wǔ jiǔ 十二点五九

6.70: liù diǎn qī 六点七

Measure Words and Money

1.

Measure words: liàngcí 量词

A measure word should be used between a number and a noun. Different measure words have different usages and should be matched to the specific object. (The good news is that you can always use the measure word "ge" instead of the others. It may not be strictly correct, and you may find people gently correct you, but you'll be understood just fine.) For more common measure words, refer to Part 2 Appendix in Book 2.

a person: yí ge rén 一个人

a cup of tea/coffee: yì bēi chá/kāfēi 一杯茶/咖啡

a glass of water: yì bēi shuǐ 一杯水

a can of beer: yí guàn píjiǔ 一罐啤酒

a bottle of red wine: yì píng hóng pútáojiǔ 一瓶红葡萄酒

(lit. a bottle red grape alcohol)

a bottle of white wine: yì píng bái pútáojiǔ 一瓶白葡萄酒

(lit. a bottle white grape alcohol)

a banana: yì tiáo xiāngjiāo 一条香蕉

a table/desk: yì zhāng zhuōzi 一张桌子

a pair of shoes: yì shuāng xiézi 一双鞋子

a room: yì jiān fángjiān 一间房间

wǒ xiǎngyào yì bēi kāfēi.

我 想要 一 杯 咖啡。

I would like a cup of coffee.

wǒ mǎi le liǎng píng hóng pútáojiǔ hé yì píng bái pútáojiǔ.

我 买 了 两 瓶 红 葡萄酒 和 一 瓶 白 葡萄酒。

I bought two bottles of red wine and one bottle of white wine.

(lit. I bought two bottles red grape alcohol and one bottle white grape alcohol.)

zhè ge fángzi yǒu liù jiān fángjiān.

这 个 房子 有 六 间 房间。

This house has 6 rooms.

2.

Several / A few / Some: jǐ 几 / yìxiē 一些

"jǐ" (several / a few) is used before a measure word.

zhè jǐ tiān / zhèxiē tiān wǒ hěn máng.

这 几 天 / 这些 天 我 很 忙。

These days I am very busy.

tā yǒu jǐ ge / yìxiē péngyǒu.

她 有 几 个 / 一些 朋友。

She has several / a few / some friends.

3.

Half: bàn 半

a half: yí bàn 一半

half an hour: bàn ge xiǎoshí 半个小时

1.5 hours: yí ge bàn xiǎoshí 一个半小时

half a month: bàn ge yuè 半个月

one and a half months: yí ge bàn yuè 一个半月

half a day: bàn tiān 半天

one and a half days: yì tiān bàn 一天半

half an apple: bàn ge píngguǒ 半个苹果

4.

Multiples of a quantity: bèi 倍

one-fold: yí bèi 一倍

(one time more than a given quantity)

two-fold: liǎng bèi 两倍

three-fold: sān bèi 三倍

jiàgé zēngjiā yí bèi le.

价格 增加 一 倍 了。

Prices have doubled.

(*lit: prices increased one-fold.*)

wǒ de shū bǐ nǐ de shū duō yí bèi.

我 的 书 比 你 的 书 多 一 倍。

I have twice as many books as you.

= wǒ de shū shì nǐ de shū de liǎng bèi.

= 我 的 书 是 你 的 书 的 两 倍。

(lit. My books than your books more one-fold. = My books are your books twice.)

5.

Discount: dǎzhé 打折 (verb), zhékòu 折扣 (noun)

In Chinese, discounts are expressed as a percentage of the original price one needs to pay, not as the percentage saved.

20% off (80% of original price): (dǎ) bā zhé (打)八折

15% off (85% of original price): (dǎ) bā wǔ zhé (打)八五折

50% off (50% of original price): (dǎ) wǔ zhé (打)五折

70% off (30% of original price): (dǎ) sān zhé (打)三折

dǎzhé ma? / yǒu zhékòu ma?

打折吗？／有折扣吗？

Do you discount? / Is there a discount?

(lit. Discount? / Have discount?)

(dǎ) jǐ zhé?

(打) 几折？

What's the discount?

(lit. How many discounts?)

jiǔ zhé.

九折。

10% off.

(lit. Nine discounts.)

6.

Money: qián 钱

Chinese currency (RMB): rénmínbì 人民币

yuan: yuán 元 (formal)

yuan: kuài(qián) 块(钱) (informal)

jiao (10 *jiao* = 1 *yuan*): jiǎo 角 (formal)

mao (= *jiao)*: máo 毛 (informal)

fen (10 *fen* = 1 *jiao*): fēn 分

50.00RMB / *yuan:* wǔshí kuài(qián) 五十块(钱)

29.90RMB / *yuan:* èrshíjiǔ kuài jiǔ (máo) 二十九块九(毛)

5.18RMB / *yuan:* wǔ kuài yì máo bā (fēn) 五块一毛八(分)

0.98RMB / *yuan:* jiǔ máo bā (fēn) 九毛八(分)

0.60RMB / *yuan:* liù máo 六毛

3.00RMB / *yuan:* sān yuán 三元 (formal)

0.80RMB / *yuan:* bā jiǎo 八角 (formal)

duōshǎo qián?

多少 钱？

How much?

(lit. How much money?)

shí'èr kuàiqián.

十二 块钱。

12RMB.

(lit. 12 piece money.)

duōshǎo qián yì jīn?

多少 钱 一 斤？

How much for half a kilo (half a kilo = 1 jin)?

(lit. How much money 1 jin?)

sān kuài wǔ yì jīn.

三块五一斤。

3.5RMB for half a kilo (half a kilo = 1 *jin*).

(lit. 3 piece 5 1 jin.)

Interrogatives

1.

Questions

Interrogative words "ma 吗" and "ne 呢"

In Chinese, "ma" and "ne" are used to form questions. They are placed at the end of a sentence. "ma" forms yes-or-no questions (except in the case "How are you?" – "nǐ hǎo ma?"). When answering these questions in Chinese, we use the same verb as the one in the question. "ne" is used to return the same question which is being discussed back to the original person.

Name,
King

nǐ shì wáng jīnglǐ ma?

你 是 王 经理 吗?

Are you the manager, Mr. Wang?

(lit. You are Wang Manager?)

shì de. / búshì.

93

是的。/ 不是。

shìde búshì

Yes, (I am). / No, (I'm not).

Lit.
Local

nǐ xǐhuān zhè ge dìfāng ma?

你 喜欢 这 个 地方 吗?

Do you like this place?

(lit. You like this place?)

wǒ xǐhuān.

我 喜欢。

Yes, I like it.

(lit. I like.)

wǒ bù xǐhuān.

我 不 喜欢。

No, I don't like it.

(lit. I not like.)

nǐ hǎo ma?

你 好 吗?

How are you?

wǒ hěn hǎo. nǐ ne?

我 很 好。 你 呢?

I'm fine. And you? / What about you?

wǒ jiào wáng lìlì. nǐ ne?

我 叫 王 丽丽。 你 呢?

My name is Wang Lili. What's yours?

2.

What: shénme 什么 什 么

What place: shénme dìfāng 什么地方 *place, space,*

HowMany

time

What time: jǐ diǎn 几点 / **shénme shíjiān** 什么时间 / **shénme shíhòu**

什么时候

shí hòu

Time, Fixed Concept of time [time and space]

The duration of time → ref hour

When: shénme shíhòu 什么时候

When (conjunction): …de shíhòu …的时候 (refer to Conjunctions

3 in this book)

nà shì shénme?

那 是 什么？

What is that?

(lit. That is what?)

would like, you want eat what

nǐ xiǎngyào chī shénme?

你 想 要 吃 什么？

What would you like to eat?

96

(lit. You would like eat what?)

zhè shì shénme dìfāng?

这 是 什么 地方?

What place is this?

(lit. This is what place?)

xiànzài jǐ diǎn? / xiànzài shì shénme shíjiān?

Justnow what time

现在 几 点? / 现在 是 什么 时间?

What time is it now?

(lit. Now what time? / Now is what time?)

Mei Guo

nǐ shénme shíhòu qù běijīng?

你 什么 时候 去 北京?

When are you going to Beijing?

(lit. You when go Beijing?)

nǐmen shénme shíhòu / jǐ diǎn qù fēijī chǎng? *Large place*

place for paticular reason

你们 什么 时候 / 几 点 去 飞机场?

What time are you going to the airport?

(lit. You what time go airport?)

3.

or shéi

Who/Whom: shuí 谁

Whose: shuí de 谁的

tā shì shuí?

他 是 谁?

Who is he?

(lit. He is who?)

nǐ gēn shuí chǎojià le?

你 跟 谁 吵架 了？

Whom/Who did you argue with?

(lit. You with whom argued?)

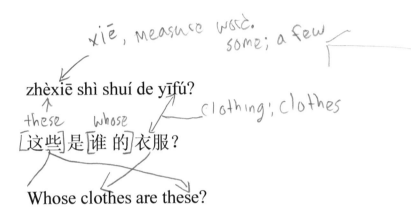

xiē, measure word.
some; a few

zhèxiē shì shuí de yīfú?

clothing; clothes

these   whose

这些 是 谁 的 衣服？

Whose clothes are these?

(lit. These are whose clothes?)

4.

Which: nǎ 哪 (singular) / nǎxiē 哪些 (plural)

nǎ ge rén zhīdào zhè ge míyǔ de dá'àn?

哪 个 人 知道 这 个 谜语 的 答案？

Which person/Who knows the key/answer to this riddle?

(lit. Which person knows this riddle's key/answer?)

píngguǒ hé chéngzi, nǐ yào nǎ yí ge? ← before nouns, without their own measure words

(handwritten: you want / which)

苹果 和 橙子，你 要 哪 一 个？

Apple or orange, which one do you want?

(lit. Apple and orange, you want which one?)

(handwritten: Which (plural))

nǐ huì tuījiàn nǎxiē cāntīng gěi wǒmen?

(handwritten: meeting; gathering; party; get together / Recommend / give; grant; present)

你 会 推荐 哪些 餐厅 给 我们？

Which restaurants will you recommend to us?

(lit. You will recommend which restaurants to us?)

5.

Where: zài nǎlǐ 在 哪里

Here: zài zhèlǐ 在 这里

There: zài nàlǐ 在 那里

nǐ zài nǎlǐ gōngzuò?

你 在 哪里 工作?

Where do you work?

(lit. You where work?)

be at, in, or on (a place)

Your

nǐ de dàxué zài nǎlǐ?

你 的 大学 在 哪里?

Where is your university?

(lit. Your university where?)

Children are there

háizimen zài nàlǐ.

孩子们 在 那里。

The children are there.

101

The children are there.

wǒ de yàoshi zài zhèlǐ.

我 的 钥匙 在 这里。

My keys are here.

6.

How: zěnme 怎么 (when preceding verbs)

How / How about: zěnmeyàng 怎么样 (when preceding verbs or at the end of the sentence)

nǐ zěnme rènshí tāmen? ("rènshí" - know (people))

你 怎么 认识 他们？

How do you know them?

(lit. You how know them?)

tā zěnme zhīdào? ("zhīdào" - know (things))

他 怎么 知道？

How does he know?

(lit. He how knows?)

shìqíng zěnmeyàng?

事情 怎么样？

How are things?

(lit. Things how?)

tāmen hǎo ma? / tāmen zěnmeyàng?

他们 好 吗? / 他们 怎么样？

How are they?

(lit. They good? / They how?)

wǒ zěnmeyàng kěyǐ dào nàlǐ?

我 怎么样 可以 到 那里？

How can I get there?

(lit. I how can get there?)

7.

How many

How many / How much: duōshǎo 多少 (small or large quantity, countable or uncountable nouns.)

How many: jǐ 几 (small quantity, countable nouns)

nǐ xiě le duōshǎo/jǐ běn shū?

你 写 了 多少/几 本 书？

How many books did you write?

(lit. You wrote how many books?)

nǐ huì zài nàlǐ dāi duōshǎo/jǐ tiān?

你 会 在 那里 呆 多少/几 天？

How many days will you stay there?

(lit. You will there stay how many days?)

duōshǎo qián?

多少 钱?

How much?

(lit. How much money?)

nǐ xiǎngyào jiā duōshǎo táng?

你 想要 加 多少 糖?

How much sugar would you like to add?

(lit. You would like add how much sugar?)

8.

Age (How old): niánlíng 年龄 / niánjì 年纪

Years old: suì 岁

nǐ jǐ suì?

你几岁?

How old are you? (when asking children)

(lit. You how many years old?)

nǐ duō dà?

你多大?

How old are you? (when asking young people)

(lit. You (how) many big?)

nín duō dà niánjì?

您多大年纪?

How old are you? (when asking old people)

(lit. You (how) many big age?)

zhè ge xiǎo nánhái sān suì.

这 个 小 男孩 三 岁。

This little boy is 3 years old.

tā èrshí suì.

她 二十 岁。

She is 20 years old.

tā wǔshíliù suì.

他 五十六 岁。

He is 56 years old.

9.

How long (time): duō jiǔ 多久

How often: duō cháng 多常

How far: duō yuǎn 多远

nǐ huì zài zhōngguó dāi duō jiǔ?

你 会 在 中国 呆 多 久？

How long will you stay in China?

(lit. You will in China stay how long?)

nǐ duō cháng qù diànyǐngyuàn?

你 多 常 去 电影院？

How often do you go to the cinema?

(lit. You how often go cinema?)

cóng zhèlǐ dào yìshù guǎn duō yuǎn?

从 这里 到 艺术 馆 多远?

How far is it from here to the Art Gallery?

(lit. *From here to the Art Gallery how far?*)

10.

How come/Why: wèishénme 为什么

Reason: yuányīn 原因

wèishéme nǐ méiyǒu gàosù wǒmen?

为什么 你 没有 告诉 我们?

Why didn't you tell us? / How come you didn't tell us?

(lit. *How come/Why you didn't tell us?*)

wèishéme nǐ zǒngshì chídào?

为什么 你 总是 迟到?

Why are you always late?

(lit. Why you always late?)

shénme yuányīn?

什么 原因?

What's the reason?

(lit. What reason?)

11.

Selective questions:

(1) Verb+不(bù)+Verb

be or not be: shì bú shì 是不是

want or not want: yào bú yào 要不要

believe or not believe: xìn bú xìn 信不信

go or not go: qù bú qù 去不去

know or not know (people): rèn bú rènshí 认不认识

know or not know (things): zhī bù zhīdào 知不知道

eat or not eat: chī bù chī 吃不吃

like or not like: xǐ bù xǐhuān 喜不喜欢

nǐ shì bú shì yīshēng? = nǐ shì yīshēng ma?

你是不是医生? = 你是医生吗?

Are you a doctor?

(lit. You are not are doctor? = You are doctor?)

nǐ rèn bú rènshí tā? = nǐ rènshí tā ma?

你认不认识他? = 你认识他吗?

Do you know him?

(lit. You know not know him? = You know him?)

111

tā zhī bù zhīdào? = tā zhīdào ma?

她 知 不 知道？＝ 她 知道 吗？

Does she know?

(lit. She knows not knows? = She knows?)

nǐ xǐ bù xǐhuān kàn diànyǐng? = nǐ xǐhuān kàn diànyǐng ma?

你 喜 不 喜欢 看 电影？＝ 你 喜欢 看 电影 吗？

Do you like watching movies?

(lit. You like not like watch movies? = You like watch movies?)

(2) 有没有 (yǒuméiyǒu) + Verb

nǐ yǒuméiyǒu kàn zhè běn shū? = nǐ kàn zhè běn shū le ma?

你 有没有 看 这 本 书？＝ 你 看 这 本 书 了 吗？

Did you read this book?

(lit. You have not have read this book? = You read this book?)

méiyǒu.

没有。

No, I didn't.

(lit. Didn't.)

nǐ yǒuméiyǒu qù jiàn tāmen? = nǐ qù jiàn tāmen le ma?

你 有 没有 去 见 他们？ = 你 去 见 他们 了 吗？

Did you go to meet them?

(lit. You have not have went meet them? = You went meet them?)

jiàn le.

见 了。

Yes, I did.

(lit. Met.)

(3) adjective + 不(bù) + adjective

right or not right: duì bú duì 对不对

good or not good: hǎo bù hǎo 好不好

tall or not tall: gāo bù gāo 高不高

happy or not happy: gāo bù gāoxìng 高不高兴

beautiful or not beautiful: piào bú piàoliàng 漂不漂亮

handsome or not handsome: shuài bú shuài 帅不帅

zhè ge dá'àn duì bú duì? = zhè ge dá'àn duì ma?

这 个 答案 对 不 对？ = 这 个 答案 对 吗？

Is this answer right?

(lit. This answer right not right? = This answer right?)

nǐ gāo bù gāoxìng? = nǐ gāoxìng ma?

你 高 不 高兴？ = 你 高兴 吗？

Are you happy?

(lit. You happy not happy? = You happy?)

tā gāo bù gāo? shuài bú shuài? = tā gāo ma? shuài ma?

他 高 不 高？ 帅 不 帅？ = 他 高 吗？ 帅 吗？

Is he tall? Is he handsome?

(lit. He tall not tall? Handsome not handsome? = He tall? Handsome?)

Prepositions

1.

"bǎ" 把

In Chinese, "bǎ" is frequently used to emphasize the object(s) in the sentence. In this sentence construction, the object is placed before the verb instead of after.

qǐng bǎ diànshì guāndiào.

请 把 电视 关掉。

Please turn off the TV.

(lit. Please bǎ TV turn off.)

wǒ bǎ suǒyǒu de língshí chī wán le.

我 把 所有 的 零食 吃 完 了。

I ate all the snacks.

(lit. I bǎ all snacks ate finished.)

tā bǎ wénjiàn fàng zài nǐ de bàngōngshì le.

他 把 文件 放 在 你 的 办公室 了。

He put the documents in your office.

(lit. He bǎ documents put in your office.)

qǐng bǎ zhuōzi hé yǐzi fàng zài yìqǐ.

请 把 桌子 和 椅子 放 在 一起。

Please put the tables and chairs together.

(lit. Please bǎ tables and chairs put together.)

2.

"by" in passive tense: bèi 被

wǒ de shǒujī bèi tōu le.

我 的 手机 被 偷 了。

My mobile phone was stolen.

(lit. My hand machine by (somebody) stolen.)

tā bèi chē zhuàng le.

他 被 车 撞 了。

He was hit by a car.

(lit. He by car hit.)

3.

In/On/At: zài 在

Same "zài" as used when currently doing something.

(1) Somebody is at someplace.

tā zài yīyuàn.

他 在 医院。

He is in the hospital.

(lit. He in hospital.)

bàozhǐ zài zhuō(zi) shàng(miàn).

报纸 在 桌(子) 上(面)。

The newspapers are on the table.

(lit. Newspapers on table up/top/above.)

wǒ zài jiā.

我 在 家。

I am at home.

(lit. I at home.)

tāmen zài bàngōngshì.

他们 在 办公室。

They are at the office.

(lit. They at office.)

(2) Somebody at some place doing something.

tā zài gōngyuán liùgǒu.

她 在 公园 遛狗。

She is walking the dog in the park.

(lit. She in park walks dog.)

tāmen zài dàxué xuéxí zhōngwén.

他们 在 大学 学习 中文。

They are learning Chinese at the university.

(lit. They at university learn Chinese.)

wǒmen zài C chūkǒu děng nǐ.

我们 在 C 出口 等 你。

We are waiting for you at Exit C.

(lit. We at C Exit wait you.)

(3)

On (the top): zài…shàng(miàn)/shàng(biān) 在…上(面)/上(边)

Under: zài…xià(miàn)/xià(biān) 在…下(面)/下(边)

In front of: zài…qiánmiàn/qiánbiān 在…前面/前边

Behind: zài…hòumiàn/hòubiān 在…后面/后边

In the east: zài…dōngmiàn/dōngbiān/dōngfāng 在…东面/东边/东方

In the west: zài…xīmiàn/xībiān/xīfāng 在…西面/西边/西方

In the south: zài…nánmiàn/nánbiān/nánfāng 在…南面/南边/南方

In the north: zài…běimiàn/běibiān/běifāng 在…北面/北边/北方

On the left: zài…zuǒbiān 在…左边

On the right: zài…yòubiān 在…右边

Opposite to: zài…duìmiàn 在…对面

māo tǎng zài shāfā shàngmiàn.

猫 躺 在 沙发 上面。

The cat is lying on the sofa.

(lit. Cat lies on sofa top.)

gǒu zài zhuōzi xiàmiàn.

狗 在 桌子 下面。

The dog is under the table.

(lit. Dog at table under.)

zài tāmen de fángzi qiánmiàn yǒu yí ge yóuyǒngchí.

在 他们 的 房子 前面 有 一 个 游泳池。

There is a swimming pool in front of their house.

(lit. In front of their house has a swimming pool.)

tāmen zhù zài zhè zuò shān de hòumiàn.

他们 住 在 这 座 山 的 后面。

They live behind this mountain.

(lit. They live at this mountain's back.)

zhōngguórén xǐhuān tāmen de fángjiān zài nánmiàn.

中国人 喜欢 他们 的 房间 在 南面。

Chinese people like their rooms facing to (lit. in) the south.

zài yínháng de yòubiān yǒu yí ge shāngdiàn.

在 银行 的 右边 有 一 个 商店。

To (lit. on) the right of the bank there is a store.

(4)

In the middle (of): zài…zhōngjiān 在…中间

Between: zài…zhījiān 在…之间

zài hú de zhōngjiān yǒu yí zuò tǎ.

在 湖 的 中间 有 一 座 塔。

There is a tower in the middle of the lake.

(lit. In the middle of lake has a tower.)

shànghǎi zài sūzhōu hé hángzhōu zhījiān.

上海 在 苏州 和 杭州 之间。

Shanghai is between Suzhou and Hangzhou.

xiǎohái zuò zài fùmǔ zhījiān.

小孩 坐 在 父母 之间。

The kid is sitting between the parents.

(5) Within: zài...zhīnèi 在...之内

wǒmen huì zài shíwǔ fēnzhōng zhīnèi dào.

我们 会 在 十五 分钟 之内 到。

We will arrive within 15mins.

(lit. We will within 15mins arrive.)

tāmen bìxū zài yí ge xīngqī zhīnèi wánchéng zhè ge xiàngmù.

他们 必须 在 一 个 星期 之内 完成 这 个 项目。

They must finish this project within a week.

(lit. They must within a week finish this project.)

4.

Come/Be from: cóng…lái 从…来 / láizì 来自…

From…to…: cóng…dào… 从…到…

nǐ cóng nǎlǐ lái?

你 从 哪里 来?

Where do you come from?

(lit. You from where come?)

wǒ cóng déguó lái.

我 从 德国 来。

I come from Germany.

(lit. I from Germany come.)

tāmen láizì měiguó.

他们 来自 美国。

They come/are from America.

dàbùfèn rén de shàngbān shíjiān shì cóng shàngwǔ jiǔ diǎn dào xiàwǔ liù diǎn.

大部分 人 的 上班 时间 是 从 上午 九 点 到 下午 六 点。

Most people's working hours are from 9a.m. to 6p.m..

(lit. Most people's working time is from late morning 9 o'clock to afternoon 6 o'clock.)

zuò fēijī cóng xiānggǎng dào lúndūn yào shí'èr ge xiǎoshí.

坐 飞机 从 香港 到 伦敦 要 十二 个 小时。

It takes 12 hours to go by plane from Hong Kong to London.

(lit. Sit plane from Hong Kong to London want 12 hours.)

5.

Be close to / Be near: lí…jìn 离…近 / kàojìn… 靠近…

127

Nearby: fùjìn 附近

Far from…: lí…yuǎn 离…远

wǒ jiā lí dàxué hěn jìn.

我 家 离 大学 很 近。

My home is very close to the university.

(lit. My home to university very close.)

tāmen de jiā kàojìn dìtiě zhàn.

他们 的 家 靠近 地铁 站。

Their home is near the subway station.

fùjìn yǒu kāfēitīng ma?

附近 有 咖啡厅 吗?

Is there a coffee shop nearby?

(lit. Nearby has coffee shop?)

jīchǎng lí zhèlǐ hěn yuǎn.

机场 离 这里 很 远。

The airport is very far from here.

(lit. Airport to here very far.)

6.

Except (excluding): chúle…zhīwài/yǐwài 除了…之外/以外

Besides (in addition to / apart from): chúle…zhīwài/yǐwài 除了…之外/以外

chúle xīngqī tiān zhīwài, tāmen měi tiān shàngbān.

除了 星期 天 之外，他们 每 天 上班。

They work every day except Sunday.

(lit. Except Sunday, they every day work / go to work.)

chúle gāngqín yǐwài, tā bú huì wán rènhé qítā yuèqì.

除了 钢琴 以外，她 不 会 玩 任何 其它 乐器。

She cannot play any musical instruments except the piano.

(lit. Except piano, she cannot play any other musical instruments.)

chúle zhōngwén yǐwài, tā yě xuéxí zhōngguó wénxué hé lìshǐ.

除了 中文 以外，她 也 学习 中国 文学 和 历史。

Besides Chinese language, she also studies Chinese literature and history.

chúle xiàtiān yǐwài, wǒmen dōngtiān yě fàngjià.

除了 夏天 以外，我们 冬天 也 放假。

Besides in the summer, we also have a vacation in the winter.

(lit. Besides summer, we winter also have a vacation.)

Conjunctions

1.

And/With: hé 和 / gēn 跟 / tóng 同 / yǔ 与

"hé" and "gēn" are more commonly used than "tóng" and "yǔ".

tā měitiān chī yí ge píngguǒ hé yí ge chéngzi.

她 每天 吃 一 个 苹果 和 一 个 橙子。

She eats an apple and (an) orange every day.

(lit. She every day eats an apple and an orange.)

nǐ kěyǐ hé/gēn wǒ yìqǐ qù.

你 可以 和/跟 我 一起 去。

You and I can go together.

(lit. You can and I together go.)

nǐ xiǎngyào hé/gēn wǒ yìqǐ qù ma?

你 想要 和/跟 我 一起 去 吗？

Would you like to go with me?

(lit. You would like with me together go?)

2.

Or: háishì 还是; huòzhě 或者

When "or" is used in a selective question (asking for a choice), its translation is "háishì". When "or" is used in a statement, it's translated into "huòzhě".

nǐ xiǎng hē chá háishì kāfēi?

你 想 喝 茶 还是 咖啡？

Do you want to drink tea or coffee?

(lit. You want drink tea or coffee?)

tā shì xuéshēng háishì lǎoshī?

她 是 学生 还是 老师？

Is she a student or a teacher?

(lit. She is student or teacher?)

míngnián nǐ huì qù ōuzhōu háishì měiguó lǚxíng?

明年 你 会 去 欧洲 还是 美国 旅行？

Will you travel to Europe or America next year?

(lit. Next year you will go Europe or America travel?)

wǒ míngtiān huòzhě hòutiān yǒu shíjiān.

我 明天 或者 后天 有 时间。

I have time tomorrow or the day after tomorrow.

(lit. I tomorrow or the day after tomorrow have time.)

tā huì qù shēnzhèn huòzhě guǎngzhōu chūchāi.

他 会 去 深圳 或者 广州 出差。

He will go on a business trip in Shenzhen or Guangzhou.

(lit. He will go Shenzhen or Guangzhou business trip.)

3.

When: …de shíhòu …的时候

When (question): shénme shíhòu 什么时候 (refer to Interrogatives 2 in this book)

wǒ zài chī wǔfàn de shíhòu, (wǒ) kàndào le tā.

我 在 吃 午饭 的 时候，(我) 看到 了 她。

I saw her when I was having lunch.

(lit. I was having lunch when, (I) saw her.)

tā wǔ suì de shíhòu xuéxí huàhuà.

她 五 岁 的 时候 学习 画画。

She learnt how to paint when she was 5 years old.

(lit. She was 5 years old when learnt paint.)

wǒ kànshū de shíhòu, jīngcháng tīng yīnyuè.

我 看书 的 时候，经常 听 音乐。

When I read, I often listen to music.

(lit. I look book when, often listen music.)

4.

...while...(doing two things at the same time): yìbiān...yìbiān... 一边...一边...

wǒmen yìbiān hē kāfēi yìbiān liáotiān.

我们 一边 喝 咖啡 一边 聊天。

We are chatting while drinking coffee.

(lit. We are drinking coffee and chatting.)

tā yìbiān shàngwǎng yìbiān kàn diànshì.

她 一边 上网 一边 看 电视。

She is watching TV while surfing the Internet.

(lit. She is surfing the Internet and watching TV.)

tā yìbiān zǒulù yìbiān tīng yīnyuè.

他 一边 走路 一边 听 音乐。

He is listening to music while walking.

(lit. He is walking and listening music)

5.

As soon as…: yī (+verb)…jiù (+verb)… 一…就…

wǒ yí dào jiù dǎ diànhuà gěi nǐ.

我 一 到 就 打 电话 给 你。

I will call you as soon as I arrive.

(lit. I as soon as arrive hit phone to/give you.)

wǒmen yí dào bàngōngshì jiù kāishǐ gōngzuò.

我们 一 到 办公室 就 开始 工作。

We start working as soon as we get to the office.

(lit. We as soon as get to/arrive office start work.)

tāmen yí dào běijīng jiù qù chángchéng.

他们 一 到 北京 就 去 长城。

As soon as they arrive in Beijing they will go to the Great Wall.

(lit. They as soon as arrive Beijing go the Great Wall.)

6.

137

Because/As: yīnwèi 因为

So: suǒyǐ 所以

"yīnwèi" (because/as) expresses a cause. "suǒyǐ" (so) expresses a result. In Chinese, they are usually used together in a sentence, but they can be also used alone.

yīnwèi tā shēngbìng le, suǒyǐ tā méiyǒu qù shàngbān.

因为 她 生病 了，所以 她 没有 去 上班。

She didn't go to work because she was sick.

(lit. Because she was sick, so she didn't go to work.)

yīnwèi tā qǐchuáng wǎn le, suǒyǐ tā cuòguò le tā de hángbān.

因为 他 起床 晚 了，所以 他 错过 了 他 的 航班。

He missed his flight because he got up late.

(lit. Because he got up late, so he missed his flight.)

tā huì shuō zhōngwén, yīnwèi tā shì zhōngguórén.

他 会 说 中文，因为 他 是 中国人。

He can speak Mandarin because he is Chinese.

wǒ zuìjìn hěn máng, suǒyǐ méiyǒu gěi nǐ dǎ diànhuà.

我 最近 很 忙，所以 没有 给 你 打 电话。

I have been busy recently, so I haven't called you.

(lit. I recently very busy, so haven't to/give you hit phone.)

7.

If: rúguǒ 如果

If...would...: rúguǒ...huì... 如果...会...

rúguǒ nǐ yǒu wèntí, nǐ kěyǐ wèn wǒ.

如果 你 有 问题，你 可以 问 我。

139

If you have questions, you can ask me.

rúguǒ jīntiān bú xiàyǔ, wǒmen huì qù páshān.

如果 今天 不 下雨，我们 会 去 爬山。

If it doesn't rain today, we will go climbing.

(lit. If today not rain, we will go climb mountain.)

rúguǒ wǒ shì nǐ, wǒ huì shì yí shì.

如果 我 是 你，我 会 试 一 试。

If I were you, I would try.

(lit. If I am you, I will try a try.)

rúguǒ tā yǒu qián, tā huì mǎi yí ge dà fángzi.

如果 他 有 钱，他 会 买 一 个 大 房子。

If he had the money, he would buy a big house.

8.

Even if: jíshǐ…yě… 即使…也…

Since: jìrán 既然

jíshǐ xiàyǔ, tāmen yě huì qù.

即使 下雨，他们 也 会 去。

They will go even if it rains.

(lit. Even if rain, they also will go.)

nà běn zìdiǎn tèbié hǎo. jíshǐ hěn guì wǒ yě huì mǎi.

那 本 字典 特别 好。即使 很 贵 我 也 会 买。

That dictionary is particularly good. Even if it is expensive I will buy it.

(lit. That dictionary particularly/espcially good. Even if very expensive I also will buy.)

jìrán nǐ bù xǐhuān nǐ de gōngzuò, nǐ yīnggāi cízhí.

141

既然 你 不 喜欢 你 的 工作，你 应该 辞职。

Since you don't like your work, you should resign.

9.

Unless...(otherwise)...: chúfēi...(yàobùrán)... 除非...(要不然)...

wǒ bùxiǎng qù, chúfēi nǐ yě qù.

我 不 想 去，除非 你 也 去。

I don't want to go unless you also go.

chúfēi tā shēngbìng le, (yàobùrán) tā huì qù shàngbān.

除非 她 生病 了，(要不然) 她 会 去 上班。

Unless she is sick, (otherwise) she will go to work.

chúfēi nǐ shì bǎiwànfùwēng, (yàobùrán) nǐ zuìhǎo bú yào qù kàn nàlǐ de fángzi.

除非 你 是 百万富翁，(要不然) 你 最好 不要 去 看 那里 的 房子。

Unless you are a millionaire, (otherwise) you'd better not go to look at the houses there.

(lit. Unless you are millionaire, otherwise you best not want go look there's houses.)

10.

Although: suīrán 虽然

But: dànshì 但是 / kěshì 可是

In Chinese, "suīrán" (although) and "dànshì/kěshì" (but) are often used together in a sentence. In English we use one or the other.

suīrán tā qīshí duō suì le, dànshì tā hěn jiànkāng.

虽然 他 七十 多 岁 了，但是 他 很 健康。

Although he is over 70, he is very healthy.

(lit. Although he 70 many years old, but he very healthy.)

suīrán dàjiā hěn lèi, kěshì hěn yúkuài.

虽然 大家 很 累，可是 很 愉快。

Everybody is tired, but happy.

(lit. Although everybody very tired, but very happy.)

tā de fángjiān bú dà, dànshì hěn zhěngjié.

她 的 房间 不 大，但是 很 整洁。

Her room is not big, but it's very tidy.

11.

Not only…but also…: búdàn…érqiě… 不但…而且…

tā búdàn huì kāichē, érqiě huì xiūlǐ.

他 不但 会 开车，而且 会 修理。

He can not only drive a car, but also repair it.

(lit. He not only can drive car, but also can repair.)

tāmen búdàn huì shuō yīngwén, érqiě huì shuō zhōngwén.

他们 不但 会 说 英文，而且 会 说 中文。

They can speak not only English, but also Chinese.

(lit. They not only can speak English, but also can speak Chinese.)

nà ge cāntīng, búdàn cài hǎochī, érqiě fúwù yě hěn hǎo.

那 个 餐厅，不但 菜 好吃，而且 服务 也 很 好。

As for that restaurant, not only is the food good, but so is the service.

(lit. That restaurant, not only the food is good eating / tasty, but also the service also/too very good.)

12.

Neither…nor…: jìbù…yěbù… 既不…也不…

tā jìbú huì tán jítā, yěbú huì tán gāngqín.

他 既 不 会 弹 吉他，也 不 会 弹 钢琴。

He can neither play the guitar nor the piano.

(lit. He neither can play guitar, nor can play piano.)

tā jìbú huì shuō yīngwén, yěbú huì shuō zhōngwén.

她 既 不 会 说 英文，也 不 会 说 中文。

She can neither speak English nor Chinese.

(lit. She neither can speak English, nor can speak Chinese.)

13.

Until: zhídào 直到

Not…until: zhídào…cái…直到…才…

Up to now: zhídào xiànzài 直到现在

So far: dào mùqián wéizhǐ 到目前为止

tā zài kànshū zhídào kāfēitīng guānmén.

她 在 看书 直到 咖啡厅 关门。

She is reading until the café closes.

zhídào huìyì wánchéng le yí bàn, tā cái lái.

直到 会议 完成 了 一 半，他 才 来。

He didn't come until the meeting was half finished.

(lit. Until meeting finished half, he only just came.)

zhídào xiànzài, wǒ hái bù zhīdào yuányīn.

直到 现在，我 还 不 知道 原因。

Up to now, I still don't know the reason.

dào mùqián wéizhǐ, wǒ fēicháng xǐhuān wǒ de gōngzuò.

到 目前 为止，我 非常 喜欢 我 的 工作。

I like my job very much so far.

(lit. So far, I very much like my job.)

Adjectives

important: zhòngyào 重要

beautiful: piàoliàng 漂亮

quiet: ānjìng 安静

comfortable: shūfú 舒服

"bù" (not) precedes an adjective for the negative forms, as in English.

not important: bú zhòngyào 不重要

not beautiful: bú piàoliàng 不漂亮

not quiet: bù ānjìng 不安静

not comfortable: bù shūfú 不舒服

When an adjective modifies a noun, "de" precedes the noun.

famous university: yǒumíng de dàxué 有名的大学

important thing: zhòngyào de shì 重要的事

beautiful girl: piàoliàng de nǚhái 漂亮的女孩

quiet place: ānjìng de dìfāng 安静的地方

comfortable sofa: shūfú de shāfā 舒服的沙发

zhèlǐ yǒu hěnduō hóngsè de huā.

这里 有 很多 红色 的 花。

There are lots of red flowers here.

(lit. Here has lots of red flowers.)

wǒmen yǒu yí ge zhòngyào de huìyì.

我们 有 一 个 重要 的 会议。

We have an important meeting.

Adjectives generally have two syllables. When no special emphasis is intended, one-syllable adjectives are usually preceded by the adverb "hěn" (very).

tā hěn gāo.

他 很 高。

He is tall.

(lit. He very tall.)

wǒ hěn hǎo.

我 很 好。

I am fine.

(lit. I very fine/good.)

zhè jiàn chènshān hěn guì.

这件衬衫很贵。

This shirt is expensive.

(lit. This shirt very expensive.)

1.

Enough: zúgòu 足够

(1) When "zúgòu" (enough) is used as an adjective to modify a noun, "de" precedes the noun.

tā méiyǒu zúgòu de qián mǎi zhè liàng chē.

他 没 有 足 够 的 钱 买 这 辆 车。

He doesn't have enough money to buy this car.

wǒ yǒu zúgòu de shíjiān gǎnshàng hángbān.

我 有 足 够 的 时间 赶 上 航班。

I have enough time to catch the flight.

bīngxiāng lǐ yǒu zúgòu de shíwù.

冰箱 里 有 足够 的 食物。

There is enough food in the fridge.

(lit. Fridge in/inside has enough food.)

(2) When "zúgòu" (enough) is used as an adverb to modify an adjective, the word order is opposite of that in English.

tāmen de fángzi zúgòu dà.

他们 的 房子 足够 大。

Their house is big enough.

(lit. Their house enough big.)

jīnnián xiàtiān zúgòu rè.

今年 夏天 足够 热。

This summer is hot enough.

(lit. This year summer enough hot.)

(3) "gòu" (enough) as an adverb is commonly used with some verbs.

Enough to eat: gòu chī 够吃

Enough to live: gòu zhù 够住

Enough to use: gòu yòng 够用

2.

Pattern: 又(yòu) + adjective +又(yòu) + adjective

wǒmen yòu è yòu kě.

我们 又 饿 又 渴。

We are hungry and thirsty.

zhèxiē lízi yòu tián yòu cuì.

这些 梨子 又 甜 又 脆。

These pears are sweet and crisp.

zhè ge xiǎonǚhái yòu kě'ài yòu guāi.

这 个 小女孩 又 可爱 又 乖。

This little girl is cute and well-behaved.

3.

Pattern (negative): 不(bù) + adjective +不(bù) + adjective

tā bú pàng bú shòu.

他 不 胖 不 瘦。

He is neither fat nor thin.

tāmen bù gāo bù ǎi.

他们 不 高 不 矮。

They are neither tall nor short.

zhè ge shāngdiàn bú dà bù xiǎo.

这 个 商店 不 大 不 小。

This shop is neither big nor small.

Comparative Degree of Adjectives

1.

A Chinese adjective doesn't change its form when being used as a comparison. **"gèng"** precedes adjectives to express comparative degree.

more: gèng 更

good: hǎo 好

better: gèng hǎo 更好

bad: chà 差 / huài 坏 / bù hǎo 不好

worse: gèng chà 更差 / gèng huài 更坏 / gèng bù hǎo 更不好

big: dà 大

bigger: gèng dà 更大

small: xiǎo 小

smaller: gèng xiǎo 更小

important: zhòngyào 重要

more important: gèng zhòngyào 更重要

2.

Than: bǐ 比

Chinese pattern: A + 比(bǐ) + B + 更(gèng) + adjective. "gèng" is placed before an adjective to emphasize the degree of difference.

wǒ bǐ wǒ jiějie gèng gāo.

我 比 我 姐姐 更 高。

I am (much/even) taller than my older sister.

(lit. I than my older sister taller.)

zhè ge bōlíbēi bǐ nà ge bōlíbēi gèng dà.

这 个 玻璃杯 比 那 个 玻璃杯 更 大。

This glass is (much/even) bigger than that one.

(lit. This glass than that glass bigger.)

wǒmen bǐ yǐqián gèng chéngshú le.

我们 比 以前 更 成熟 了。

We are (much/even) more mature than before.

(lit. We than before more mature.)

3.

As...as...: hé...yíyàng... 和...一样...

Chinese pattern: A + 和(hé) + B + 一样(yíyàng) + adjective

tā hé wǒ yíyàng gāo.

她 和 我 一样 高。

She is as tall as me.

(lit. She and I the same tall.)

nǐ de bèibāo hé tā de bèibāo yíyàng zhòng.

你 的 背 包 和 他 的 背 包 一 样 重。

Your backpack is as heavy as his.

(lit. Your backpack and his backpack the same heavy.)

4.

When comparing the action of A and the action of B, the verb should follow A.

(1) Chinese pattern: A + verb + 得(de) + 比(bǐ) + B + 更(gèng) + adverb

tā pǎo de bǐ tā de péngyǒu gèng kuài.

他 跑 得 比 他 的 朋 友 更 快。

He runs (much) faster than his friend.

(lit. He runs than his friend faster.)

tā xiě de bǐ wǒ gèng duō.

她 写 得 比 我 更 多。

She wrote more than me.

(lit. She wrote than me more.)

(2) Chinese pattern: A + verb + 得(de) +和(hé) + B + 一样(yíyàng) + adverb

tā pǎo de hé tā de péngyǒu yíyàng kuài.

他 跑 得 和 他 的 朋 友 一 样 快。

He runs as fast as his friend.

(lit. He runs and his friends the same fast.)

tā xiě de hé wǒ yíyàng duō.

她 写 得 和 我 一 样 多。

She wrote as much as me.

(lit. She wrote and me the same many.)

Superlative Degrees of Adjectives

1.

"zuì" is placed before the adjective to create the superlative degree.

the best / the most: zuì 最

the best: zuì hǎo 最好

the worst: zuì chà 最差 / zuì huài 最坏 / zuì bù hǎo 最不好

the biggest: zuì dà 最大

the smallest: zuì xiǎo 最小

the most beautiful: zuì piàoliàng 最漂亮

tā shì wǒ zuì hǎo de péngyǒu.

她 是 我 最 好 的 朋友。

She is my best friend.

163

zhè shì zuì guì de chènshān.

这 是 最 贵 的 衬衫。

This is the most expensive shirt.

jīntiān shì wǒ zuì máng de yì tiān.

今天 是 我 最 忙 的 一 天。

Today is my busiest day.

(lit. Today is my busiest one day.)

2.

Favorite: zuì xǐhuān de 最喜欢的

nǐ zuì xǐhuān shénme shuǐguǒ?

你 最 喜欢 什么 水果?

= nǐ zuì xǐhuān de shuǐguǒ shì shénme?

= 你 最 喜欢 的 水果 是 什么？

= shénme shì nǐ zuì xǐhuān de shuǐguǒ?

= 什么 是 你 最 喜欢 的 水果？

What's your favorite fruit?

(lit. You best/most like what fruit? = You best/most like's fruit is what?
= What is you best/most like's frut?)

wǒ zuì xǐhuān de shuǐguǒ shì pútáo.

我 最 喜欢 的 水果 是 葡萄。

= pútáo shì wǒ zuì xǐhuān de shuǐguǒ.

= 葡萄 是 我 最 喜欢 的 水果。

My favorite fruit is grapes.

(lit. I best/most like's fruit is grapes. = Grapes are I best/most like's
fruit.

báisè shì wǒ zuì xǐhuān de yánsè.

白 色 是 我 最 喜欢 的 颜色。

White is my favorite color.

zhè bú shì wǒ zuì xǐhuān de T xù.

这 不 是 我 最 喜欢 的 T 恤。

This is not my favorite T-shirt.

3.

more and more: yuèláiyuè... 越来越...

"yuèláiyuè..." (more and more) precedes the adjective and follows the subject to express the growing degree of a situation.

Chinese pattern: S + 越来越(yuèláiyuè) + adjective

tāmen yuèláiyuè máng.

他们 越来越 忙。

They are getting busier and busier.

shíwù yuèláiyuè guì.

食物 越来越 贵。

Food is more and more expensive.

tiānqì yuèláiyuè lěng.

天气 越来越 冷。

The weather is getting colder and colder.

4.

The more…the more…: yuè…yuè… 越…越…

(1) When "yuè…yuè…" (the more…the more…) modifies a verb, it expresses the idea that the quantity is increasing.

Chinese pattern: S + 越(yuè) + verb1 + 越(yuè) + verb2

háizimen yuè chī yuè xiǎng chī.

孩子们 越 吃 越 想 吃。

The more the children eat, the more they want.

(lit. Children the more eat the more want eat.)

wǒ yuè kàn yuè xǐhuān zhè běn xiǎoshuō.

我 越 看 越 喜欢 这 本 小说。

The more I read, the more I like this novel.

(lit. I the more read the more like this novel.)

(2) Chinese pattern: S + 越(yuè) + verb + 越(yuè) + adjective/adverb

tā yuè chī bīngqílín yuè pàng.

他 越 吃 冰淇淋 越 胖。

The more he eats ice cream, the fatter he gets.

(lit. He the more eats ice cream the fatter.)

tā yuè shuō yuè kuài.

她 越 说 越 快。

The more she speaks, the faster she speaks.

(lit. She the more speaks the faster.)

(3) When "yuè…yuè…" (the more…the more…) modifies an adjective, it expresses the result of a situation.

Chinese pattern: S + 越(yuè) + adjective 1 + 越(yuè) + adjective 2

wǒmen yuè máng yuè luàn.

我们 越 忙 越 乱。

The busier we are, the messier it is.

(lit. We the busier the messier.)

yīfú yuè piányi zhìliàng yuè bù hǎo.

衣服 越 便宜 质量 越 不 好。

The cheaper the clothes (are), the lower the quality (is).

(lit. Clothes the cheaper quality the not better.)

Common Adjectives and Their Related Words

1.

Early: zǎo 早

Late: chídào 迟到 / wǎn 晚

Delay: wǎndiǎn 晚点

duìbùqǐ, wǒ chídào le.

对不起，我 迟到 了。

Sorry, I am late.

wǒ huì chídào shíwǔ fēnzhōng. / wǒ huì wǎn dào shíwǔ fēnzhōng.

我 会 迟到 十五 分钟。 / 我 会 晚 到 十五 分钟。

I will be 15 minutes late. / I will arrive 15 minutes late.

(lit. I will late 15 minutes. / I will late arrive 15 minutes.)

tā zǎo dào le bàn ge xiǎoshí.

他 早 到 了 半 个 小时。

He arrived half an hour early.

(lit. He early arrived half an hour.)

míngtiān wǒ xūyào zǎo qǐchuáng.

明天 我 需要 早 起床。

I need to get up early tomorrow.

(lit. Tomorrow I need early get up.)

huǒchē wǎndiǎn le.

火车 晚点 了。

The train is delayed.

2.

Funny: yǒuqù 有趣

Funny (informal): hǎoxiào 好笑 / gǎoxiào 搞笑

Kidding/Joking: kāi wánxiào 开玩笑

To play a joke on (somebody): gēn…kāi wánxiào 跟…开玩笑

Meaning: yìsī 意思

Interesting *(lit. have meaning)***: yǒuyìsī 有意思**

Be interested in…: duì…gǎn xìngqù 对…感兴趣

tāmen hěn yǒuqù.

他们 很 有趣。

They are very funny.

zhè ge gùshì hěn hǎoxiào.

这 个 故事 很 好笑。

This story is very funny.

nǐ zài kāi wánxiào!

你 在 开 玩笑 !

You are kidding/joking!

tā de gēgē xǐhuān gēn tā kāi wánxiào.

他 的 哥哥 喜欢 跟 他 开 玩笑 。

His older brother likes to play jokes on him.

(lit. His older brother likes with him joking.)

wǒ zhīdào nǐ de yìsī.

我 知道 你 的 意思 。

I know what you mean.

(lit. I know your meaning.)

zhè ge zhǔyì hěn yǒuyìsī.

这 个 主意 很 有意思。

This idea is very interesting.

(lit. This idea very has meaning.)

tā duì shùxué gǎn xìngqù.

他 对 数学 感 兴趣。

He is interested in math.

(lit. He in math interested.)

wǒ duì zhè jiàn shì bù gǎn xìngqù.

我 对 这件 事 不 感 兴趣。

I am not interested in this matter.

(lit. I in this matter not interested.)

3.

Be satisfied with: mǎnyì 满意 / duì…(gǎndào) mǎnyì 对…(感到) 满意 (about quality)

Be satisfied with: mǎnzú 满足 / duì…(gǎndào) mǎnzú 对…(感到) 满足 (about quantity)

lǎobǎn bù mǎnyì tāmen de gōngzuò.

老板 不 满意 他们 的 工作。

= lǎobǎn duì tāmen de gōngzuò (gǎndào) bù mǎnyì.

= 老板 对 他们 的 工作 (感到) 不 满意。

The boss is not satisfied with their work.

(lit. Boss not satisfied their work. = Boss with their work (feels) not satisfied.)

gùkè duì zhè ge cāntīng de fúwù (gǎndào) hěn mǎnyì.

顾客 对 这 个 餐厅 的 服务 (感到) 很 满意。

Customers are very satisfied with the service in this restaurant.

(lit. Customers with this restaurant's service (feel) very satisfied.)

tā bù mǎnzú tā yǐjīng yǒu de chéngjì.

他 不 满足 他 已经 有 的 成绩。

= tā duì tā yǐjīng yǒu de chéngjì (gǎndào) bù mǎnzú.

= 他 对 他 已经 有 的 成绩 (感到) 不 满足。

He is not satisfied with the achievements he has already made *(lit. had).*

(lit. He not satisfied he already has' achievements. = He with he already has' achievements (feel) not satisfied.)

4.

Easy: róngyì 容易

Simple: jiǎndān 简单

jiějué zhè ge wèntí bù róngyì.

解决 这 个 问题 不 容易。

It's not easy to solve this problem.

(lit. Solve this problem not easy.)

tāmen xǐhuān jiǎndān de shēnghuó.

他们 喜欢 简单 的 生活。

They like simple life.

5.

Good to eat / Delicious / Tasty: hǎo chī 好吃

Good to drink: hǎo hē 好喝

Good to listen / Sounds good: hǎo tīng 好听

Good to watch/look: hǎo kàn 好看

Good to play / Fun: hǎo wán 好玩

Not good to eat: bù hǎo chī 不好吃 / nán chī 难吃 *(lit. hard/difficult eat)*

Not good to listen to / Sounds bad: bù hǎo tīng 不好听 / **nán ting** 难听 *(lit. hard/difficult listen)*

Not good to watch/look: bù hǎo kàn 不好看 / **nán kàn** 难看 *(lit. hard difficult watch/look)*

Not good to play / Not fun: bù hǎo wán 不好玩

diǎnxīn hěn hǎo chī.

点心 很 好 吃。

Dim Sum is very good (tasty) to eat.

(lit. Dim Sum very good eat.)

bái pútáojiǔ hěn hǎo hē.

白 葡萄酒 很 好 喝。

The white wine is very good (delicious) to drink.

(lit. White wine very good drink.)

yǒuxiē gǔdiǎn yīnyuè tèbié hǎo tīng.

有些 古典 音乐 特别 好 听。

Some classical music sounds especially good.

(lit. Some classical music especially good listen.)

bǐsài hǎo kàn ma?

比赛 好 看 吗？

Was the match good to watch?

(lit. Match good watch?)

shàng ge zhōumò wǒmen qù le zhǔtí gōngyuán. zhēn hǎo wán!

上 个 周末 我们 去 了 主题 公园。真 好 玩！

We went to the theme park last weekend. It was really fun!

(lit. Last weekend we went theme park. Really good play!)

zhè ge cāntīng de cài bù hǎo chī.

这 个 餐厅 的 菜 不 好 吃。

The food in this restaurant is not delicious.

(lit. This restaurant's food/dishes not good eat.)

zhè shǒu gē bù hǎo tīng.

这 首 歌 不 好 听。

This song is not good to listen to / sounds bad.

(lit. This song not good listen.)

zuótiān wǎnshàng de diànyǐng zhēn nán kàn.

昨天 晚上 的 电影 真 难 看。

The movie last night was really not good to watch.

(lit. Last night's movie really hard/difficult watch.)

xiànzài qù yóuyǒng bù hǎo wán. yóuyǒngchí yǒu tài duō rén le.

现在 去 游泳 不 好 玩。游泳池 有 太 多 人 了。

It's not fun to go swimming now. There are too many people in the pool.

(lit. Now go swimming not good play. Swimming pool has too many people.)

6.

Be good at…: shàncháng… 擅长… / hěnhuì… 很会…

tā shàncháng tī zúqiú.

他 擅长 踢 足球。

He is good at playing *(lit. kicking)* football.

zhè ge xiǎo nǚhái shàncháng/hěnhuì jiǎng gùshì.

这 个 小 女孩 擅长/很会 讲 故事。

This little girl is good at telling stories.

tā shàncháng/hěnhuì jiǎng xiàohuà.

他 擅长/很会 讲 笑话。

He is good at telling jokes.

7.

Be afraid/scared of: pà 怕 / hàipà 害怕

Be afraid that + sentence: kǒngpà 恐怕

Be terrified / Be filled with terror: kǒngjù 恐惧

Frightening: kěpà 可怕

Horrible/Terrible / Horror (movie): kǒngbù 恐怖

To scare: xià 吓

tā pà gǒu.

她 怕 狗。

She is afraid of dogs.

tài àn le. tā hěn hàipà.

太 暗 了。她 很 害怕。

It's too dark. She is very afraid/scared.

kǒngpà wǒ bāng bùliǎo nǐ.

恐怕 我 帮 不 了 你。

I am afraid that I am unable to help you. (…bùliǎo, refer to BOOK 2 "Common Verbs and Their Usages" 35)

(lit. Afraid I help not you.)

kǒngpà míngtiān huì xiàyǔ.

恐怕 明天 会 下雨。

I am afraid that it will rain tomorrow.

(lit. Afraid tomorrow will rain.)

tīngdào SARS de bàodào, dàjiā dōu hěn kǒngjù.

听到 SARS 的 报道，大家 都 很 恐惧。

Everyone was terrified / filled with terror when hearing the report about SARS.

(lit. Hear SARS' report, everyone all very terrified.)

zhànzhēng zhēn kěpà.

战争 真 可怕。

The war is really frightening.

tā shì yí ge kǒngbù de rén.

他 是 一 个 恐怖 的 人。

He is a horrible person.

wǒ bù xǐhuān kàn kǒngbù diànyǐng.

我 不 喜欢 看 恐怖 电影。

I don't like to watch horror movies.

nǐ bié xià wǒ, hǎo bù hǎo?

你 别 吓 我, 好 不 好?

Don't scare me, ok?

(lit. You don't scare me, ok not ok?)

nǐ xià sǐ wǒ le.

你 吓 死 我 了。

You scared me to death.

(lit. You scared death me.)

8.

Many: hěn duō 很多

Some of / A part of: yí bùfèn 一部分

Most of: dà bùfèn 大部分

zhuōzi shàng yǒu hěnduō shū.

桌子 上 有 很多 书。

There are many books on the desk.

(lit. Desk up has many books.)

yí bùfèn xuéshēng zài chànggē.

一 部分 学生 在 唱歌。

Some of the students are singing.

(lit. A part students are singing.)

wǒ de dà bùfèn péngyǒu zài zhè ge chéngshì gōngzuò.

我 的 大 部分 朋友 在 这 个 城市 工作。

Most of my friends work in this city.

(lit. My big part friends in this city work.)

9.

Whole: zhěng 整

All: quánbù de 全部的 / suǒyǒu de 所有的

(1) "zhěng" (whole) is used with a measure word to modify a noun. "quánbù de" (all) and "suǒyǒu de" (all) are used to modify nouns as subjects or objects. The adverb "dōu" (all) can be added to follow the subject.

zhěng ge fángjiān luànqībāzāo.

整 个 房间 乱七八糟(idiom)。

The whole room is messy.

(lit. Whole room messy seven eight bad.)

tāmen quánbù dōu zài zhèlǐ gōngzuò.

他们 全部 都 在 这里 工作。

They all work here.

(lit. They all all here work.)

quánbù de shū dōu shì xīn de.

全部 的 书 都 是 新 的。

All the books are new.

(lit. All books all are new.)

tāmen qù guò suǒyǒu de zhèxiē dìfāng.

他们 去 过 所有 的 这些 地方。

They have been to all these places.

(lit. They have been all these places.)

nà ge cāntīng de suǒyǒu de cài dōu tài xián.

那 个 餐厅 的 所有 的 菜 都 太 咸。

In that restaurant, all of the dishes are too salty.

(lit. That restaurant's all dishes all too salty.)

(2) Commonly used expressions with "quán" (all):

all of the family / the whole family: quán jiā 全家

all of the class / the whole class: quán bān 全班

the whole country: quán guó 全国

the whole body: quán shēn 全身

full name: quán míng 全名

10.

Wrong: cuò 错

Mistake: cuò 错 / cuòwù 错误

Fault: cuò 错 / guòcuò 过错

tā gěi le nǐ yí ge cuò de diànhuà hàomǎ.

他 给 了 你 一 个 错 的 电话 号码。

He gave you a wrong phone number.

tāmen fàn le yí ge dà de cuò / cuòwù.

他们 犯 了 一 个 大 的 错 / 错误。

They made a big mistake.

(lit. They committed a big mistake.)

shì wǒ de cuò / guòcuò.

是 我 的 错 / 过错。

It is my fault.

Well-done! BOOK 1 is finished!

Step by Step: mànmàn lái / yí bù yí bù lái 慢慢来 / 一步一步来

Other books in the series by Vivienne Zhang:

Modern Chinese (BOOK 2)

– Learn Chinese in a Simple and Successful Way – Series BOOK 1, 2, 3, 4

Modern Chinese (BOOK 3)

– Learn Chinese in a Simple and Successful Way – Series BOOK 1, 2, 3, 4

Modern Chinese (BOOK 4)

– Learn Chinese in a Simple and Successful Way – Series BOOK 1, 2, 3, 4

Made in the USA
San Bernardino, CA
19 November 2019